The Paradox of the American Metropolis

The Paradox of the American Metropolis

. . .

Alan Rabinowitz

The Paradox of the American Metropolis

ISBN 13: 9781534615564
ISBN: 1534615563

Published by Quansoo Press
3400 East Laurelhurst Drive, Seattle WA 98105
206-525-7941

To all those citizen activists, in this era of urban growth and climate change and search for fairness, who will finally get their state legislatures to insist that their local governments work together for the common good of their metropolises.

Contents

Prologue

. . .

THIS BOOK IS A LAST hurrah for the city as we have known it and a belated greeting for the metropolis that replaces it as the context for our urban existence.

The paradox in any given metropolis in America is that both state legislators and local officials are elected by the same group of voters. On the one hand, metroscale problems call for solutions that are largely under the legislature's control, but the state legislators are hesitant to take necessary steps to restructure local governments. On the other hand, elected local officials are usually focused on protecting their fiefdoms and have equally great difficulty in working with each other on the metroscale problems of their jurisdiction.

You and I—citizens, voters, urbanites—want safe and equitable communities to live in. However, to get them we must break the impasse that the paradox has created and that emerged in the post–World War II era as a majority of Americans ended up living in urban areas. A majority of urbanized Americans now live in the suburbs of central cities and thus are in a position to make sure that a majority of state legislators are respectful of their likes and dislikes, which unfortunately are often racist and exclusionist in essence.

In short, my potentially activist or already-activist readers should come to understand that "metropolis" has literally replaced "city" as the main conception of an urban environment. American metropolises are chock-full of autonomous local governments no more willing to be herded than cats. We in America have emphasized decentralized democratic decision-making about these issues, in sharp contrast to the top-down manner by which urban government is handled in other nations. The major exception in the United States is the authoritarian manner in which most state-level departments of transportation utilize federal Highway Trust Funds.

Metropolises, it is widely noted, are idiosyncratic, necessary, subject to influence by citizens but politically unorganized, and are now required to deal with worldwide increases in urban population and climate change. Air and water pollution, racial injustice, housing, transportation, economic development, pollution control, schools, climate-change preparedness and so many other facets of urban life are problems best tackled and resolved at the level of the metropolis. But a metropolitan area in the United States is composed of a central city and a score or more of local general governments plus any number of independent school districts and special districts with taxing power. A large metro area may have over a thousand such governmental units. It is no wonder that it is difficult for citizens to figure out how to deal with all the different pieces that make up the whole of a metropolis.

Local governments in the United States are basically creatures of their state legislatures, which can create them and change their boundaries and powers to tax as often as they please, with no possibility of appeal to a higher authority or court. This is the dictum made by Judge Dillon in the nineteenth century, as examined in more detail in chapter 2. Changes in the relations between local and state authorities require the enthusiastic participation of the general taxpaying public; no big changes in state and local government are possible without a vast amount of grassroots support for them.

At the very least, I hope this essay will provide some interesting knowledge and, more importantly, generate additional grassroots activism to improve conditions in our metropolitanized society. It reflects my experience of teaching graduate courses in urban economics and planning as a professor at the University of Washington, on top of a lifetime working in and around what I sometimes call urban capitalism. The underlying characteristic of the material in this essay, however, has to do with electoral politics—which, in its way, acknowledges the work of Harvard professor V. O. Key, who had a scholarship named after him at the MIT-Harvard Joint Center for Urban Studies, the scholarship I had for writing my PhD dissertation at MIT.

<u>A university is a world full of footnotes, but, for this essay, I do not provide any footnotes at all because I believe there is sufficient reference to United Nations and domestic source material in the text</u>. For excerpted quotations in indented paragraphs, notably about conditions in other countries and about leading Supreme Court cases, attribution is made in the text to area studies by the Library of Congress as well as eponymous articles in *Wikipedia* and elsewhere on the Internet.

Step by step over the past two hundred years or so, the impacts of those Supreme Court decisions are primary reasons why we, the people, now have the ultimate responsibility for doing something to minimize our individual and collective impact on the environment and to maximize our satisfaction with urban life. We have to do whatever it is we do in a world that is being forced to accept the reality of climate change even as populations continue to grow and flow into megacities and metropolises. The abiding challenge is to think clearly about how we ordinary people can use our power to produce desirable changes at the level of the metropolis, an amorphous entity with magnetic attraction for all who care about the ecological and social health of our urban environments.

CHAPTER 1

Metropolises Today and Tomorrow, Here and Abroad

• • •

DEFINITIONS

EVERY REASONABLY CIVIC-MINDED AMERICAN KNOWS, more or less, how to deal with his or her own local government. However, the majority of all Americans nowadays live in a metropolis, and here most people are stumped, for probably there is no single governmental agency—or set of agencies—responsible for what goes on. Nevertheless, we all need to deal with the metropolitan dimension in our life as the urban population in the United States steadily continues to grow.

Urban populations grow at even higher rates abroad than here, and administration of local urban areas abroad is far more centralized than in the United States. The basic democratic nature of our governmental systems means that comprehensive planning for any given metropolis is an unlikely outcome of our attempts to comprehend, encompass, manage, and stabilize our metropolises. But I believe ultimately we can do an adequate job of self-government, including the ability to concoct prescriptions for our own locale's metropolis.

Thus let us begin with a few kudos for the very existence and unscripted character of metropolises in American urban life. We celebrate the democratic nature of the metropolises of America with full understanding that democracy often leads to institutional chaos and disparate governance—more specifically, that the elected officials of the local governments in a given metropolitan area have almost never been enthusiastic about working together.

The self-governing character of American localities is in contrast to what happens in the rest of the world as populations continue to rise and rates of urbanization increase even faster. Learned articles, government agencies, and the news media shed their lights on an emerging group of so-called megacities. From our point of view, their use of the term "megacity" to describe a region-sized complex of residential, commercial, and industrial areas and areas for educational, religious, recreational, and transportational activities and the arts is merely recognition of the fact that all sizable cities are ipso facto metropolises. In short, the old concept of the city has been transcended and is obsolete and misleading.

Governance of localities is difficult at best. Virtually all the other nations govern their localities in autocratic and authoritarian ways, keeping local governments in thrall to the national government and limiting their independent access to fiscal resources. In many developing countries, a majority of the population is crowded into one or two urban areas. See the Appendix for a birds'-eye view of how other nations deal with their local governments. The Appendix provides some evidence that the United States really is unique among the nations of the world in regard to the care and management of its local civic base. Central governments in sixteen representative countries have the power to make decisions for their localities and provide much of the financing for local operating programs on an annual basis. By contrast, in the United States, only a few federal and state-level agencies have important influence over local conditions.

As one examines the metropolises of America, the term "unruly" may come to mind, a term that my ancient *Webster's Seventh New Collegiate Dictionary* aptly says means "Not readily ruled, disciplined, or managed: turbulent." Among its synonyms, says the dictionary, are Ungovernable, Intractable, and Refractory. The definition continues: "UNRULY suggests a lack of or incapacity for discipline; UNGOVERNABLE implies not being subdued or restrained or an escape from guidance or control; INTRACTABLE suggests stubborn resistance to guidance or control; refractory stresses resistance to attempts to manage or to mold."

All those adjectives apply to every metropolis in the United States, and that suits our national image of ourselves just fine. Beyond such self-satisfaction lies a history of many centuries of working out processes for governance at local, state, and federal levels. The next chapter of this essay considers some of the elements of these processes that date from the early nineteenth century and explains why decision-making about the metropolis is so decentralized in America.

The essential step in beginning to think as clearly as one can about metropolitan phenomena in America and elsewhere is to accept the indeterminate and indefinable character of the array confronting you. The implication of dealing with a fuzzy set of characteristics of a given metropolis is that any attempt to construct a representative sample of a group of metropolises that could provide the analyst with a set of "currently useful generalizations" for comparison would, however, then be denigrated by statistical purists.

Throughout this essay (and equally in the real world of city halls, state legislatures, and federal offices), the words used to define and describe metropolis are indeterminate and indefinable, like the ones below. Except for certain clearly definable items such as a statute mile, all of the entities that describe the domains where people live are idiosyncratic. No two metropolises are alike; what lies within the borders of a given metropolis, assuming there is agreement as to where the borders are, may have scant similarity to the insides of other metropolises nearby. One learns to live with such ambiguities and immeasurables. My comments on a few familiar terms follow:

Metropolis. My dictionary says that the etymological root of "metro" is "mother." I rather like that, for it conveys the spirit of a given metropolis giving life and shape to a given urbanized environment.

City. I do not think that the US Congress has ever defined a city. That duty is left to state legislatures, of which we now have fifty, each promulgating its own hierarchy of local governments for places to be called county, city, town, village, and hamlet. And each state legislature (according to the Dillon Rule to which I subscribe and which is described in the next chapter) is free to change definitions at will.

Suburban. This denotes a particular part of a metropolis with lower density than the so-called central city with which it is associated—except that in many metropolises, suburbs have become far more built up for commerce as well as residential use than they were, while suburban governments are jointly and sometimes severally as powerful as the central cities they abut. In the United States, a majority of people living in urban areas live in the suburbs rather than in central cities, and putative solutions to environmental and racist issues necessarily challenge the mind-sets of suburban residents.

Exurban. This describes an area with even lower densities, lying on the fringe of the urbanized area being analyzed, presumably beyond any boundaries that have been established to limit urban growth but still within the stated boundaries of the metropolis itself.

Urban agglomerations. This is a term used often in United Nations publications and in the realm of regional science. Agglomerations, however, continue to be referred to as cities, even though in reality they are metropolises. Cities with 10 million or more residents are now being referred to as "megacities."

Urban. This is in contrast to rural. Our federal government calls any settlement with a population of 2,500 or more as urban for the purposes of the census. The UN report cited in the next section begs the issue of defining urban because it varies so much across the globe.

Adopting a common language for the concepts and terms to be used in concocting a decision-making system for a given metropolis seems like a useful first step for its policymakers, journalists, and citizens. The second step, of course, is to recognize that cities everywhere have metamorphosed into more complex metropolitan forms that, most often, contain a variety of old-fashioned cities within their boundaries. These two steps are mental gyrations that are low-tech in the extreme, but they quite possibly represent the biggest impediments to creative thinking about the present and the future for the people in any given metropolis on this planet.

WORLDWIDE URBAN-POPULATION TRENDS

In all the ways that matter, local areas in the United States appear to be governed differently from local areas in virtually every other nation. Indeed, American metropolises compete with metropolises and megacities across the globe, so it is fitting, before going on with our own experience in America, to explore the differences between our system and that of other nations in this era in which we are expecting metropolitan areas to keep on growing and growing.

It is widely assumed, quite properly, that the urban population will increase in every nation in the next few decades. The ultimate source of data pertaining to total world population and its urban and rural components is the Department of Economic and Social Affairs of the United Nations Secretariat. The data it collects and analyses are the foundation for most of the observations made about changes in the world that are brought about by increases in numbers of people, technological changes, and the politics of particular places.

Most of the data and excerpts in this chapter come from the "Highlights of the 2014 Revision" to its World Urbanization Prospects reports (UN Dept. of Economic and Social Affairs, Population Division, Publication ST/ESA/SER. A/352). Let us begin by noting that the UN counted twenty-nine megacities (urban agglomerations with populations over 10 million) in the world in 2014, including six in Asia, three in the Americas (north and south), one in North Africa, and twelve other agglomerations. Among the global trends noted in the 2014 report:

* Globally, more people live in urban areas than in rural areas, with 54 percent of the world's population in urban areas in 2014. In 1950, 30 percent of the world's population was urban, and, by 2050, 66 percent of the world's population is projected to be urban.
* The urban population of the world has grown rapidly since 1950, from 746 million to 3.9 billion in 2014.
* The rural population of the world has grown slowly since 1950 and is expected to reach its peak in a few years. The global rural population is now close to 3.4 billion and is expected to decline to 3.2 billion by 2050.

More particularly, looking at the urbanization trends by region that are estimated by the UN to show the basic pattern of current world development, the North America region, including Canada and Mexico, was quite urbanized back in 1990 (75 percent) and is expected to become even more so by 2050, rising to 87 percent. Europe would go from 70 percent in 1990 to 82 percent in 2050, and Latin America would go from 71 percent to 82 percent in that same period. Africa and Asia will almost double their degree of urban population by 2050, from 31 percent and 32 percent in 1990 to 56 percent and 64 percent respectively.

There are different theories and practices that characterize development programs in the present era. The basic pattern reflected above is dissected in the many volumes that have been written about the elements of urbanization, about the economic and social transformations that it creates, and about the policies that help a given country to produce (in the words of the 2014 UN report) "urban development that integrates all facets of sustainable development, to promote equity, welfare, and shared prosperity in an urbanizing world." It is always important to be respectful of efforts to define and measure the phenomena of urbanism, but, at the same time, everyone should learn to be cautious of the results, partly because (again in the words of the UN report),

> *There is no common global definition of what constitutes an urban settlement. As a result, the urban definition employed by national statistical offices varies widely across countries, and in some cases has changed over time within a country. The criteria for classifying an area as urban may be based on one or a combination of characteristics, such as: a minimum population threshold; population density; proportion employed in non-agricultural sectors; the presence of infrastructure such as paved roads, electricity, piped water or sewers; and the presence of education or health services.*

Definitions and data for areas in the United States are subject to exactly the same sort of caveats. And the same degree of variation and difficulty in being precise about any aspect of urban life (in the United States and elsewhere) applies to data concerning city and metropolitan population size. Again, from the UN report:

> *In compiling information on city population size, the Population Division has endeavored to use data or estimates based on the concept of urban agglomeration. When these data are not consistently available, population data that refer to the city as defined by its administrative boundaries were used. However, when the administrative boundaries of cities remain fixed for long periods of time, they are likely to misrepresent the actual growth of a city with respect to both its territory and its population. For a number of cities, the data available refer to two concepts: the city proper as defined by administrative boundaries and its metropolitan area. In those instances, the data referring to the metropolitan area were usually preferred because they are thought to approximate better the territory associated with the urban agglomeration. For any given city, an effort was made to ensure that the time series of population estimates derived from national sources conforms to the same definition over time. Adjustments were made when necessary to achieve internal consistency.*

The inexorable increase in population across the world affects urban trends or practices in the United States (where rates of growth in its various areas are projected somewhat lower for the future than was true in the past century). Cities with 10 million or more residents are now being referred to as "megacities." Knowing about megacities is important, but we must not neglect the hundreds of smaller "urban agglomerations" that do not get the coverage in the media that the megacities get. The UN report notes:

Megacities are notable for their size and concentration of economic activity, but are home to only about one in eight of the world's urban dwellers. In 1990 there were 10 "megacities," home to 153 million people, representing less than 7 per cent of the global urban population. Today [2014], the number of megacities has nearly tripled to 28, the population they contain has grown to 453 million, and these agglomerations now account for 12 per cent of the world's urban dwellers.

Tokyo is the world's largest city with an agglomeration of 38 million inhabitants, followed by Delhi with 25 million, Shanghai with 23 million, and Mexico City, Mumbai, and Sao Paulo, each with around 21 million inhabitants. By 2020, Tokyo's population is projected to begin to decline, although it will remain the world's largest agglomeration in 2030 with 37 million inhabitants, followed closely by Delhi, whose population is projected to rise swiftly to 36 million. While Osaka (Kinki Major Metropolitan area) and New York-Newark were the world's second and third largest urban agglomerations in 1990, by 2030 they are projected to fall in rank to the 13th and 14th positions, respectively.

The UN report includes population data for seventy-one areas with more than 5 million people. Here are more data for the top ten, with special attention to be paid concerning the extent to which the population of a whole country in clustered around a central metropolis: **Tokyo**, Japan, ranked first, where 37.8 million is 30 percent of the nations' population; **Delhi**, India, ranked second, where 25.0 million is only 2 percent of the nation's population; **Shanghai**, China, ranked third, where 23.0 million is 2 percent of the nation's population; **Mexico City**, Mexico, ranked fourth, where 20.8 million is 17 percent of the nation's population; **Sao Paulo**, Brazil, ranked fifth, where 20.8 million is 10 percent of the nation's population; **Mumba**i, India, ranked sixth, where 20.7 million is 2 percent of the nation's population; **Kinki,** Japan, ranked seventh, where 20.1 million is 16 percent of the nation's population; **Beijing**, China, ranked eighth, where 19.5 million is 1 percent of the nation's population; **NY-Newark**, USA, ranked ninth, where 18.6 million is 6 percent of the nation's population; and **Cairo**, Egypt, ranked tenth, where 18.4 million is 22 percent of the nation's population.

New York-Newark is the only US area in the top ten megacities. The United States has one other megacity with a population over 10.0 million: **Los Angeles**, USA, ranked twentieth, where its 12.3 million is 4 percent of the nation's population. There are five US cities in next grouping, populations between 5.0 and 10.0 million, shown here with two major capitol areas: **Moscow**, Russia, ranked twenty-first, where 12.1 million is 8 percent of the nation's population; **Paris**, France, ranked twenty-fifth; its 10.8 million is 17 percent of the nation's population; **Chicago**, USA, ranked thirty-seventh, where 8.7 million is 3 percent of the nation's population; **Miami**, USA, ranked fifty-eight, where 5.8 million is 2 percent of the nation's population; **Philadelphia**, USA, ranked sixty-second, where 5.6 million is 2 percent of the nation's population; **Houston**, USA, ranked sixty-fifth, where 5.6 million is 2 percent of the nation's population; **Atlanta**, USA, ranked seventy-first, where 5.0 million is 2 percent of the nation's population.

Learning how the nations listed above deal with their megacities and larger metropolises would merit a bevy of PhD dissertations in the field of comparative government, but that level of knowledge is beyond our need or scope in this essay. We are thus limited to the information currently available, which is usually presented in one of two main forms: an article (or book) that describes the chaotic atmosphere of crude settlements with too many dislocated people and few basic urban services, such as sewers, water supply, hospitals, paved roads, stores, schools, and even electricity; or an article (or book) that shows a variety of design solutions for one or another of the problems that overpopulation brings to a metropolis and its congeries of independent municipalities.

What we do know is that the old concept of city is obsolete and misleading and that all these urban conditions and possibilities must be dealt with in the language of metropolises. So who has the power to guide this process of transformation from city-level thinking to metro-level thinking? How are we to foster community democracy as local groups shape their methods of participating in metro-level decision-making?

The short answer is that the power we speak of resides somewhere far above the level of local governing institutions—somewhere in the country's federal structure. Some form of federalism is required to manage a country. Some new forms of local or subregional institutions have to be created to enable a process of decision-making by state, local, and national governments to go forward.

We can picture the typical megacity as a beehive of activities situated between an array of disconnected local governments and a central government composed of a set of ministries with various powers over the local and regional units of government. The point here is that the ideal dialogue in a federalist system assumes a balance, however ambiguous and never-to-be resolved, between central government and the local powers. But in most of the world, the powers of the central ministries far outweigh that of the locals.

No information is presented in the UN report about the hundreds or thousands of urban agglomerations with less than 5 million inhabitants, but there is certainly an understanding that almost all of these smaller places are growing in their individual and idiosyncratic ways (except for a few areas in the United States and elsewhere that have lost their economic bases). And each agglomeration, large and small, has to be dealt with, even though the term "governed" may be too strong a description of the degree of oversight that the growth process deserves.

One might be somewhat surprised to find New York-Newark listed as the only US area in the list of ten largest megacities in 2014 and not at all surprised to find its ranking drop by the year 2030. By 2030, only fifteen years into the future, the UN expects there to be forty megacities, with the top ten composed of seven in Asia, two in Africa (Cairo and Lagos), and one in the Americas (Mexico).

In 2014 six major US agglomerations (Atlanta, Miami, Los Angeles, Philadelphia, Houston, and Chicago) and three important European capitals (Moscow, London, and Paris) were in the second tier of megacities, those with 5 million or more but less than 10 million in population.

None of the handful of the so-called megacities in the United States is held responsible to or subject to unified superior governmental power. Each is impacted by the processes of the federal government, the several states and thousands of general governments and special districts that, taken together, exercise local government power (including the power to raise revenue by taxes) in United States. The creation and current application of those diffuse powers are the subjects of the remaining chapters in this essay.

By comparison, local governments in literally all other countries are subject to rules and regulations set by national ministries, which provide most of the revenues for the support of their local governments.

CHAPTER 2

How The United States Developed its Federalism and Its Community Democracy

• • •

THE EXTRAORDINARY IDEA THAT CITIZENS were entitled to a say in governmental activities permeated the variety of cities, counties, and provinces or states that coalesced to form the Continental Congress in the pre-Revolution days in the late eighteenth century, And so, from our origins, we experienced government significantly differently from our cousins in England and the rest of Europe.

Disclosure: many of the ideas and examples in this chapter and its fascinating story come from materials I developed as a professor of urban planning at the University of Washington, for a course designed to inculcate into students some appreciation of the law as it pertained to the theory and practice of city and regional planning—or, as the English put it, town and country planning. **In the paragraphs below, summaries of US Supreme Court decisions come from articles in _Wikipedia_ under the name of the case.**

And, of course, one begins with a look at the thirteen English colonies in North America, out of which our nation was crafted. By the end of the seventeenth century, England had control of all the Atlantic areas and had induced Dutch, Swedish, and other interested parties to relinquish their interests. The grants and charters had begun to merge into a basic pattern that recognized a monarch in England who appointed a governor for each colony or province. Each of these states had a legislature locally elected rather than appointed. The pattern prevailed when Georgia and the Carolinas became colonies in the early eighteenth century. Each of the thirteen colonies had its own story of creating a new art of self-government, out of which eventually grew the idea of independence from England and the subsequent development of a union of the thirteen states. These stories merge to constitute our nation's birthing story, part of an exploration of the processes that still govern how Americans can go about controlling their metropolitanized world.

The truly original part of the story is that we began our collective history with a dedication to the power of the people to own a voice in governance, by means of a state-wide, locally elected legislature to counter the power of the monarchy and its governor. The typical state was created after settlements had become organized into city form. The state would be composed of counties, whose primary function was operating a judicial system, and the counties would have autonomous towns or small cities. The legislature would be drawn from the property-owning voters (not, at the time, a very diverse group). Often the counties preceded establishment of the state itself.

None of the nations abroad that we survey in the Appendix had such a real and emotional investment in autonomous local governance. The history of European cities as they emerged from the church-led feudal era includes, for instance, the creation of Hanseatic League city-states run by their guilds on the reasonable premise that it was a sufficient forum to represent their citizenry. But more often, as nation-states emerged across Europe, the central government held the power over a hierarchy of regional counties or provinces, with cities at the bottom of the pyramid.

The US Constitution, in contrast, starts at the bottom with "We the People" electing the state legislatures. The federal constitution leaves all matters pertaining to the operation and financing of the state and its sheaf of local governments to the state. As one consequence, we have fifty slightly different arrangements. The Eleventh Amendment to the Constitution merely says that no state can be sued on its debt without its permission—an amendment that, in due course, changed the nature of our local governments.

As discussed below, a driving force in the writing of the federal and state constitutions is the promotion and protection of economic development by the private sector.

The first half of the nineteenth century, before the Civil War, saw a number of controversies get resolved in ways that affected the shapes and activities of substate governments and corporate entities, and some of these matters rose to the level of the US Supreme Court. The issues treated are interwoven with each other and are resonant in today's political discourses: creating the corporate form, taxation, debt, and many aspects of the laws pertaining to land use and corporate power.

But these ancient conflicts and resolutions also provide the framework for tackling the need for public guidance and control of expanding metropolises in the present day, recognizing that the metropolis is made up of scores of independent general governments (such as towns and cities), hundreds, even thousands of special governmental creations (such as fire districts, libraries, mosquito control districts, etc.), numberless private corporations and private landowners and millions of people making use of buildings and land already regulated and taxed by the various governmental entities.

The corporation itself was a rather revolutionary concept in those early days. The newly fashioned private corporation provided a means for people to merge their interests and protect themselves from legal suits in order to undertake larger scale activities than were easily provided by the prevailing forms of partnerships and individual entrepreneurships. At the same time, new forms of municipal or public corporations were evolving to provide a platform for the efforts of citizens to manage their public domains by themselves where such management had been in the hands of churches, guilds, or noble families.

The stories presented below (with many abstracts from *Wikipedia* articles) represent significant steps in the process of change as the years rolled by after the US Constitution took effect in 1789 and as the assortment of governments in the new federalist system explored the boundaries of their relationships with each other and with the private corporations. All this in the name of and in the search for economic stability and growth.

Steps in the Process:

The New England states, early in the nineteenth century, were forced to accept the notion that they could not leave the union because certain national policies would have negative effects on their economies.

The Hartford Convention was a series of meetings from December 15, 1814–January 5, 1815 in Hartford, Connecticut, United States, in which the New England Federalist Party met to discuss their grievances concerning the ongoing War of 1812 and the political problems arising from the federal government's increasing power. Despite radical outcries among Federalists for

New England secession and a separate peace with Great Britain, moderates outnumbered them and extreme proposals were not a major focus of the debate...

The convention discussed removing the three-fifths compromise which gave slave states more power in Congress and requiring a two-thirds super majority in Congress for the admission of new states, declarations of war, and laws restricting trade. The Federalists also discussed their grievances with the Louisiana Purchase and the Embargo of 1807. However, weeks after the convention's end, news of Major General Andrew Jackson's overwhelming victory in New Orleans swept over the Northeast, discrediting and disgracing the Federalists, resulting in their elimination as a major national political force.

The federal government was forced to give up the idea of being the nation's engine of development as proposed by Albert Gallatin, secretary of the treasury, in 1808.

In 1808 Gallatin proposed a dramatic $20 million program of internal improvements—that is, roads and canals along the Atlantic seacoast and across the Appalachian mountain barrier to be financed by the federal government. This was something new, and many considered it outright unconstitutional. It was *rejected by the "Old Republican" faction of his party that deeply distrusted the national government, and anyway there was no money to pay for it. Most of Gallatin's proposals were eventually carried out years later, but this was done not by the concerted federal action he proposed but by local governmental and private action. Though often wasteful, this method enlisted local and private energies in large enterprises.*

The state legislatures had to give up the idea that a private corporation would forever be subject to legislative review of its operations and possible revocation of its charter: *Trustees of Dartmouth College v. Woodward*, 1819.

The legal structure of the modern U.S. business corporation had its genesis in Trustees of Dartmouth College v. Woodward, 17 U.S. (4 Wheat.) 518, 4 L. Ed. 629 (1819), which held that private corporate charters are protected from state interference by the Contracts Clause of the U.S. Constitution (art. I, § 10)...

Dartmouth College was founded in 1769 by Reverend Eleazer Wheelock as a school for missionaries and Native Americans...In 1769, Wheelock obtained a corporate charter from the royal governor of New Hampshire. The charter outlined the governing structure of the school, including the English and colonial boards of trustees...In December 1816, the legislature passed a law that renamed the college Dartmouth University and made it a public school controlled by a state-appointed governing board.

Given the horrific impact on American political life of the Supreme Court's upholding the idea that private corporations are fictitious persons and are entitled to the protection of the First Amendment, as most recently exemplified in the Citizen United doctrine in relation to campaign finance, the decisions in the Dartmouth College case turned out to be extraordinarily prescient.

Marshall's opinion defined a corporation as "an artificial being, invisible, intangible, and existing only in contemplation of law." According to the Court, a corporation possesses only the properties and powers conferred upon it by law. Dartmouth College was a corporation and, as a party to the contract created by the charter, could enforce its constitutional right to be free from impairment of its obligation.

The Dartmouth College case had far-reaching implications. By establishing that private corporate charters are contracts protected by the Constitution, this decision enabled business corporations to operate under whatever terms are dictated in their charters, without fear of interference by the state. This freedom was an important agent in the enormous growth of corporations in the nineteenth and early twentieth centuries, a necessary adjunct to the development of the U.S. econo-my. In addition, the case was the first to recognize that a corporation is a "person" for legal purposes, able to sue and be sued. It also established the principle that vested property rights, such as those granted in a cor-porate charter, fall within the purview of the Contracts Clause. By so doing, the decision established that the Contracts Clause protects the right to acquire and dis-pose of property. This protection, in turn, encouraged economic venture and development.

States had to give up the idea that they could increase their revenue by taxing federal property. *McCulloch v. Maryland*, 1819

In the landmark Supreme Court case McCulloch v. Maryland, Chief Justice John expansion of Federal power. This case involved the power of Congress to charter a bank, which sparked the even broader issue of the division of powers between state and the Federal Government.

In 1816 Congress established the Second National Bank to help control the amount of unregulated currency issued by state banks. Many states questioned the constitu-tionality of the national bank, and Maryland set a prec-edent by requiring taxes on all banks not chartered by the state. In 1818 the State of Maryland approved legislation to impose taxes on the Second National Bank chartered by Congress...

James W. McCulloch, a Federal cashier at the Baltimore branch of the U.S. bank, refused to pay the taxes imposed by the state. Maryland filed a suit against McCulloch in an effort to collect the taxes. The Supreme Court, however, decided that the chartering of a bank was an implied power of the Constitution, under the "elastic clause," which granted Congress the authority to "make all laws which shall be necessary and proper for carrying into execution" the work of the Federal Government.

This case presented a major issue that challenged the Constitution: Does the Federal Government hold sovereign power over states? The proceedings posed two questions: Does the Constitution give Congress power to create a bank? And could individual states ban or tax the bank? The court decided that the Federal Government had the right and power to set up a Federal bank and that states did not have the power to tax the Federal Government. Marshall ruled in favor of the Federal Government and concluded, "the power to tax involves the power to destroy."

The private corporations had to realize that they could not stop needed public facilities from being built. *Charles River Bridge v. Warren Bridge*, 1837

The 1837 decision in *The Proprietors of Charles River Bridge, Plaintiffs in Error v. The Proprietors of Warren Bridge, and others* was:

> *That the Massachusetts state legislature's decision to grant a charter to the proprietors of Warren Bridge after granting a similar charter to the Charles River Bridge Company did not constitute a violation of the Contract Clause...*
>
> *In 1785, the Charles River Bridge Company had been granted a charter to construct a bridge over the Charles River connecting Boston and Cambridge. When the Commonwealth of Massachusetts sanctioned another company to build the Warren Bridge, chartered 1828, that would be very close in proximity to the first bridge and would connect the same two cities, the proprietors of the Charles River Bridge claimed that the Massachusetts legislature had broken its contract with the Charles River Bridge Company, and thus the contract had been violated. The owners of the first bridge claimed that the charter had implied exclusive rights to the Charles River Bridge Company. The Court ultimately sided with Warren Bridge...*
>
> *The bridge was a giant success. It made large profits and proved to be very convenient. In 1828, a company was given the rights to build the Warren Bridge, which would be extraordinarily close to the Charles River Bridge. The Warren Bridge would be turned over to the state once enough tolls had been collected*

to pay for the bridge's construction, or after a maximum of 6 years, after which it would be free to the public. Since it was free, and so close to the Charles River Bridge, the Warren Bridge would obviously take all of the competing bridge's traffic, and therefore its construction would leave the stock of the Charles River Bridge highly devalued and the shareholders would stand to lose a great deal of money...

In his opinion, [Chief Justice] Taney argued that the case was strictly about interpretation of contract, and that the charter contract should be interpreted as narrowly as possible, which meant that the Charles River Bridge did not have exclusive rights. He also stated that, in general, public grants should be interpreted closely and, if there is ever any uncertainty in a contract, the decision made should be one to better the public. He said, "While the rights of private property are sacredly guarded, we must not forget that the community also have rights, and that the happiness and well-being of every citizen depends on their faithful preservation." In his remarks, Taney also explored what the negative effects on the country would be if the Court had sided with the Charles River Bridge Company. He stated that had that been the decision of the Court, transportation would be affected around the whole country. Taney made the point that with the rise of technology, canals and railroads had started to take away business from highways, and if charters granted monopolies to corporations, then these sorts of transportation improvements would not be able *to flourish. If this were the case then, Taney said, the country would "be thrown back to the improvements of the last century, and obliged to stand still."*

A note on the transformation of American law from English Common Law to encourage private investment:

As Taney pointed out, the coming of canals and railroads and the clearing of forests and plains for agriculture was changing the industrial/commercial landscape and, as Morton Horwitz wrote in his monumental work on the requirements for progress in this area, among the changes were insulation of railroads from suits concerning cows frightened by railroad noises and forest fires started by railroad engines, together with recodification of water rights to shield land developments upstream from suits by people downstream whose flow of water was being affected. The main argument of his book is that in the first half of the nineteenth century, many judges self-consciously allied themselves with a rapidly growing class of mercantile capitalists and promoted a series of legal rules which favored those capitalists. His first book, *The Transformation of American Law, 1780–1860*, was published in 1977 and is widely regarded as one of the most important books in modern American legal historiography. It won the Bancroft Prize, the preeminent prize in American history in the United States.

The pages above provide examples of how government of local areas was being formed to accommodate economic expansion. The basic organization confronting state power was the corporation, both private and municipal. The basic fuel for building infrastructure (primarily those canals, railroads, and turnpikes) for this emerging economy was debt issued by states, especially in the years following the evident success of the Erie Canal which opened in 1825. A severe test of the viability of the economic system that resulted from all this building activity came in 1837, as described below.

Panic of 1837

The Panic of 1837 was a financial crisis in the United States that touched off a major recession that lasted until the mid-1840s. Profits, prices, and wages went down while unemployment went up. Pessimism abounded during the time. The panic had both domestic and foreign origins. Speculative lending practices in western states, a sharp decline in cotton prices, a collapsing land bubble, international specie flows, and restrictive lending policies in Great Britain were all to blame. On May 10, 1837, banks in New York City suspended specie payments, meaning that they would no longer redeem commercial paper in specie at full face value. Despite a brief recovery in 1838, the recession persisted for approximately seven years. Banks collapsed, businesses failed, prices declined, and thousands of workers lost their jobs. Unemployment may have been as high as 25% in some locales. The years 1837 to 1844 were, generally speaking, years of deflation in wages and prices.

The crisis followed a period of economic expansion from mid-1834 to mid-1836. The prices of land, cotton, and slaves rose sharply in these years. The origins of this boom had many causes, both domestic and international. Because of the peculiar factors (Specie Circular) of international trade at the time, abundant amounts of silver were coming into the United States from Mexico and China. Land sales and tariffs on imports were also generating substantial federal revenues.

Through lucrative cotton exports and the marketing of state-backed bonds in British money markets, the United States acquired significant capital investment from Great Britain. These bonds financed transportation projects in the United States. British loans, made available through Anglo-American banking houses like Baring Brothers, fueled much of the United States's westward expansion, infrastructure improvements, industrial expansion, and economic development during the antebellum era.

In 1836, directors of the Bank of England noticed that the Bank's monetary reserves had declined precipitously in recent years, possibly because of poor wheat harvests that forced Great Britain to import much of its food...

> *[For a number of reasons] The Bank of England raised interest rates, major banks in the United States were forced to do the same...Many individual states defaulted on their bonds, which angered British creditors. For a brief time, the United States withdrew from international money markets. Only in the late-1840s did Americans re-enter these markets. These defaults, along with other consequences of the recession, carried major implications for the relationship between the state and economic development.*

For this essay, the important thing is that after the fallout from the Panic of 1837, no private investor or bank would buy bonds issued by states unless the state agreed to be willing to be sued on its debt, as outlined in the Eleventh Amendment. Gone were the British banks—Barings in particular—that had bought state bonds for the building of railroads. As a result, it turned out that some internal improvements could be financed by counties and municipalities, giving these formerly quiescent local units of government powers never before imagined. And thus it was that counties and cities became important actors in the metropolitan level we look at here.

In any case, an abiding question: do local governments have inherent powers to operate without explicit sanction by a state legislature?

Competing judgments in the latter part of the nineteenth century by judges Dillon and Cooley made the nation confront basic questions concerning the power of states to control the local governments that they had created and the power of local governments to do whatever they could. The *Wikipedia* article quotes David Y. Miller's argument that Dillon had hit upon a central paradox defining American cities: having great political authority while having little legal legitimacy. He quotes Dillon as calling municipalities "mere tenants at will of their respective state legislatures" which could be "eliminated by the legislature with a stroke of the pen." Dillon also said that eliminating local government would be "so great a folly, and so great a wrong."

Thomas McIntyre Cooley (1824–1898) was a chief justice of the Michigan Supreme Court, dean of the University of Michigan Law School until 1884, and first chairman of the Interstate Commerce Commission (1887).

John Forrest Dillon (1831–1914) was an American jurist who served on federal and Iowa state courts. While on the federal bench, Dillon wrote *Municipal Corporations* (1872), one of the earliest systematic studies of the subject. After leaving the Circuit Court, Dillon was a professor at Columbia Law School from 1879 until 1882, where he taught real estate and equity. He taught at Yale Law School from 1891 until 1892, during which time he also served as the president of the American Bar Association. Dillon then returned to private practice until his death.

The theory of state preeminence over local govern-ments was expressed as Dillon's Rule in an 1868 case: "Municipal corporations owe their origin to, and derive their powers and rights wholly from, the legislature. It breathes into them the breath of life, without which they cannot exist. As it creates, so may it destroy. If it may destroy, it may abridge and control."

The Cooley Doctrine expressed the theory of an inherent right to local self-determination...[Where Dillon's Rule] posits that towns and cities have no in-dependent authority except as explicitly or implicitly granted by a state legislature) the Cooley Doctrine pro-posed a legal theory of an inherent but constitutionally-permitted right to local self-determination...Cooley, J., wrote in People v. Hurlbut "local government is [a] mat-ter of absolute right; and the state cannot take it away."

In his treatise *The General Principles of Constitutional Law in the United States of America*, on the subject of municipal corporations, Cooley wrote:

It is axiomatic that the management of purely local affairs belongs to the people concerned, not only because of being their own affairs, but because they will best understand, and be most competent to manage them. The continued and permanent existence of local gov-ernment is, therefore, assumed in all the state consti-tutions, and is a matter of constitutional right, even when not in terms expressly provided for. It would not be competent to dispense with it by statute.

• • •

The Dillon Rule

In Municipal Corporations (1872), Dillon explained that in contrast to the powers of states, which are un- limited but for express restrictions under the state or federal constitution, municipalities only have the pow- ers that are expressly granted to them. This formula- tion of the scope of municipal power came to be known as the Dillon Rule: that municipal governments have only the powers expressly granted to them by the state legislature, those that are necessarily implied from that grant of power, and those that are essential and indispensable to the municipality's existence and func- tioning; that any ambiguities in the legislative grant of power should be resolved against the municipality so that its powers are narrowly construed; that when the state has not specifically directed the method by which the municipality may implement its granted power, the municipality has the discretion to choose the method so long as its choice is reasonable.

Hundreds of U.S. court decisions have employed the Dillon Rule to determine the scope of municipal powers and rights. Critics of the rule have argued that it imposes unreasonable constraints on the ability of communities to govern themselves and undermines democracy or that local self-government is a matter of natural right that does not need to be conferred by higher political structures. Some have suggested that Dillon's approach derived from the contemporary view that cities were inherently corrupt political organs. Deviations from the Dillon Rule remain in the minority, however, despite the significant decrease in the public perception of municipal corruption.

The Supreme Court of the United States cited Municipal Corporations and fully adopted Dillon's emphasis on state power over municipalities in Merrill v. Monticello, which upheld the power of Pennsylvania to consolidate the city of Allegheny into the city of Pittsburgh, despite the objections of a majority of Allegheny's residents. The Court's ruling that states could alter or abolish at will the charters of municipal corporations without infringing upon contract rights relied upon Dillon's distinction between public, municipal corporations and private ones.

And then, the rise of "public" utilities

The thirty-five years from the end of the Civil War to the beginning of the twentieth century added new dimensions to the role of local substate governments in the federal system. It was already established that many of these substate units could borrow money and issue bonds for economic development projects, that private corporations could play a role, and that there were limits to what legislatures could do to interfere with corporations that had been properly chartered.

All of the substate governments were constituted as municipal corporations. The Cooley/Dillon arguments continued to fly back and forth, but the object of possible funding had moved on from the railroads and canals of the antebellum years to an endless set of gas, electric, and water facilities. The prevailing doctrine was against direct ownership by the municipal corporations in favor of a new form of private corporation, the privately owned "public utility" regulated by government to assure the public is being served in good order.

Note that there was important symbiosis during these last decades of the nineteenth century between the business world that was slowly being dominated by financial houses and the new world of professional economics; the American Economic Association had just been founded and its main subjects had to do with the economics of public utilities, the same being true of the newly established departments of [municipal] economics in the leading universities.

A note on the coming of special districts

The acknowledged pioneer of municipal corporations with responsibilities beyond city limits was the Boston Metropolitan Parks Commission, set up by the Massachusetts legislature in 1892 with three trustees appointed by the legislature:

> *The improvement of areas of undeveloped land, detrimental development, and polluted land in and around Boston for a system of interconnected parks was first conceived and promoted by landscape architect Charles Eliot and Sylvester Baxter, a Boston newspaper writer and city planning enthusiast. Eliot had apprenticed with Frederick Law Olmsted and later assumed leadership of Olmsted's design firm in 1893...In 1919, the commission was renamed the Metropolitan District Commission (MDC) after merging with the Metropolitan Water and Sewer Commission.*

The MDC was precursor of thousands of special districts that are festooned in and around America, from rural areas to central cities. Special districts as defined for the US Census of Governments are "All organized local entities (other than counties, municipalities, townships, or school districts) authorized by state law to provide only one or a limited number of designated functions, and with sufficient administrative and fiscal autonomy to qualify as separate governments; known by a variety of titles, including districts, authorities, boards, and commissions. In 2012 the Census reported 51,146 special-purpose districts and 12,880 independent school districts (not part of general governments) in the United States compared to 90,056 general-purpose governments.

It should be no surprise that some of the larger metropolises in the United States contain hundreds, even thousands of special districts, all of which have to be integrated into the planning agendas of the metropolis. Typically the directors are appointed by the general governments served by the special-purpose district, and usually the district has the power to get the revenue it needs by levying a tax on the residents of the district being served.

In a number of major urban areas (such as Washington DC, San Francisco, Chicago, Boston and New York), a major supporting and goading role may be played by private groups of citizens. The first great example at the metropolitan scale is the Regional Plan of New York.

In 1922, some of New York's most prominent business and professional leaders joined forces to launch an ambitious effort to survey, analyze and plan the future growth of the metropolitan region...

This initiative was the first to recognize a New York metropolitan region—one that encompassed New Jersey and Connecticut. The results of this effort were the publication in 1929 of the landmark "Regional Plan of New York and Its Environs," the first long-range, region-wide master plan for the New York metropolitan region, and the formation of the Regional Plan Association, an organization whose purpose at the time was to see that the plan was implemented.

Developing long-range regional plans remained a core focus of the organization over the next nine decades, and it remains a key part of the organization's role today. Yet over the years, long-range plans have come to represent only a fraction of RPA's work. Since the 1930s, RPA has conducted groundbreaking research on issues of land use, transportation, the environmental, economic development and opportunity. It also has led advocacy campaigns in support of the organization's goal of fostering a thriving, diverse and environmentally sustainable region.

Disclosure: I worked for the RPA in the mid-1950s.

Shortly before the RPA began its work, the Port of New York Authority (PONYA) was created and became exceptionally vital as implementer of RPA plans for transportation improvements that would serve the entire metropolis as RPA defined it.

The Port of New York Authority was established on April 30, 1921, through an interstate compact between the states of New Jersey and New York. This was the first such agency in the United States, created under a provision in the Constitution of the United States permitting interstate compacts. The idea for the Port Authority was conceived during the Progressive Era, which aimed at the reduction of political corruption and at increasing the efficiency of government. With the Port Authority at a distance from political pressures, it was able to carry longer-term infrastructure projects irrespective of the election cycles and in a more efficient manner. In 1972 it was renamed the Port Authority of New York and New Jersey to better reflect its status as a partnership between the two states.

Throughout its history, there have been concerns about democratic accountability, or lack thereof at the Port Authority...At the beginning of the 20th century, there were no road bridge or tunnel crossings between the two states...Using its ability to issue bonds and collect revenue, the Port Authority has built and managed major infrastructure projects [including the ill-fated World Trade Center]...In 1942, Austin J. Tobin became the Executive Director of the Port Authority...

Members of the Board of Commissioners are typically business titans and political power brokers who maintain close relationships with their respective Governors...Financially, the Port Authority has no power to tax and does not receive tax money from any local or state governments. Instead, it operates on the revenues it makes from its rents, tolls, fees, and facilities.

A question arose in the late 1930s as to whether the Port Authority of New York was in essence a nongovernmental enterprise whose payments of interest on its bonds should be considered as taxable as those of any completely private corporation. It had no power to tax. It had been a pioneer among toll-bridge owners in rejecting the precept that tolls should be removed as soon as the initial capital costs of the project were recaptured and its bond issues retired; instead the Port Authority used profits from one project to finance the next one. It had the power of eminent domain, as did many railroads and public utilities, and its own police force.

The case reached the federal circuit court of Justice Learned Hand who rendered the majority opinion that the Port Authority was actually a special kind of municipal corporation, interest on whose bonds should be exempt from federal taxation, just as cities and counties were. On the strength of this decision, a whole new set of income-producing "special districts" and authorities sprang up across the county in the post–World War II period. Based on the PONYA model, toll bridges, turnpikes, parking facilities, airport terminals, freight terminals, and many other public enterprises, many immune from electoral politics and few with the power of taxation to offer as security for their borrowings, have effectively changed the intergovernmental framework of metropolitan areas in ways that might not have been possible had they not been deemed public in nature.

By the time of the New Deal, the importance of the substate world of local governments was recognized. See *Our Cities: Their Role in the National Economy*, a report of the Urbanism Committee of the National Resources Committee, 1937, all with a keen sense of the way in which, even then, metropolitanism was overwhelming the old central city nexus. The WPA (Works Progress Administration) meanwhile was setting its troops of unemployed town planners and architects to work mapping so-called blighted areas in these metropolises and sketching out highways...

As World War II came to America in the late 1930s and early 1940s, the federal government began supporting a variety of industries—munitions, tanks and airplanes, freighters, and materiel of all sorts—but required that they be located in suburbs rather than in central cities; naturally this also bred a strong need for access highways, housing for war workers, and other forms of infrastructure, and set the suburbs up to receive most of the economic growth that characterized the postwar period. As a result, by the end of the war, the demand arose for government assistance for central cities, leading eventually to the Housing Act of 1949 and the Urban Redevelopment and later Urban Renewal programs. The bulk of new housing, based on the GI Bill, however, was in the suburbs, which, unfortunately, were basically unfriendly to nonwhites, a set of attitudes that fed the emotions underlying the civil rights movement and the passage of various antidiscrimination laws.

A note on defining the metropolis

At last we get to thinking about how metropolitan areas were defined by the federal government (and reflected in academic circles). The following paragraphs are a pastiche of text in governmental publications, beginning in

1964 and getting more and more complex as the national population grew and changed in the decades thereafter:

The concept of "Standard Metropolitan Statistical Areas" has been developed to meet the need for the presentation of general-purpose statistics by agencies of the Federal Government, in accordance with specific criteria for defining such areas. On the basis of these criteria, "definitions" of the areas in terms of geographic boundaries are established by the Bureau of the Budget with the advice of the Federal Committee on Standard Metropolitan Statistical Areas, which is composed of representatives of the major Federal statistical agencies.

Standard definitions of metropolitan statistical areas were first issued in 1949 as "Standard Metropolitan Areas." They were developed to replace four different sets of definitions then in use for various statistical purposes: "metropolitan districts," "metropolitan counties," "industrial areas," and "labor market areas." Because of the use of these different definitions, it was not possible to relate the statistics on population, industrial production, labor force, and other series for the area in question, since each series included a slightly different territory...

The general concept of a metropolitan area is one of an integrated economic and social unit with a recognized large population nucleus. To serve the statistical purposes for which metropolitan areas are defined, their parts must themselves be areas for which statistics are usually or often collected. Thus, each standard metro-politan statistical area must contain at least one city of at least 50,000 inhabitants...

In 2016 we are blessed with a hierarchy of areal types as defined by the Office of Management and Budget—altogether 1098 in number, more or less as follows:

- 541 Micro Statistical Areas (µSAs), alongside
- 588 Metropolitan Statistical Areas (MSAs), both of which may find themselves in
- a Core Based Statistical Area (CBSA), some of which may be combined into
- a Combined Statistical Area.

Note: previous terms that are no longer used include standard metropolitan statistical area (SMSA) and primary metropolitan statistical area (PMSA). In New England, towns have precedence over counties, so statistically similar areas are defined in terms of town-based units known as New England city and town areas (NECTAs).

A final comment by the OMB (Office of Management and Budget, Executive Office of the President) ties all of the concern about the size, shape and viability of our galaxy of metropolitan types into the consideration of activities in other countries around the globe:

The close relationship between large linked metropolitan regions and a nation's ability to compete in the global economy is recognized in Europe and Asia. Each has aggressively pursued strategies to manage projected population growth and strengthen economic prosperity in its large regions.

The European Spatial Development Perspective, a set of policies and strategies adopted by the European Union in 1999, is working to integrate the economies of the member regions, reduce economic disparities, and increase economic competitiveness...

In East Asia, comprehensive strategic planning for large regions, centered on metropolitan areas, has become increasingly common and has progressed further than in the United States or Europe. Planning for the Hong Kong-Pearl River Delta region, for instance, aims to enhance the region's economic strength and competitiveness by overcoming local fragmentation, building on global economic cooperation, taking advantage of mutually beneficial economic factors, increasing connectivity among development nodes, and pursuing other strategic directions.

At this point we can return to the question as to what American citizen activists can do and ought to be doing to improve livability and equity inside their particular metropolitan area in this era of deep concern about climate change and global warming.

CHAPTER 3

A Citizen's Approach to the Metropolitan Complex

• • •

WE ARE JUSTLY PROUD THAT we have fifty states that are more or less sovereign, over three thousand counties with many of them part of over one thousand metropolitan areas, and, altogether about ninety thousand general governments (all of them subject to electoral processes) and sixty-four thousand independent schools and various kinds of special districts. Our national mantra is that it is up to voters to mandate governmental change by getting the right people into office, especially in reference to state and local legislators. As Judge Dillon says (see Chapter Two), the powers of substate governments are ultimately determined by state legislatures; and significant changes can only be ordained by them.

But, in the meantime, there is a host of worthwhile activities for citizens to pursue to set the stage for intelligent response to global warming, on the one hand, and to economic competition in both national and international arenas, on the other. In the paragraphs below, I outline a few such approaches, painfully aware that no one person can fully comprehend all the issues that are relevant, and even citizens working together can rarely do more than create pressure on political decision-makers.

A good first step here is to think about information:

* Every metropolis, large and small, needs to have an effective data-crunching agency to process the truly vast amount of information available from the US Census and other federal and state agencies about a given area. Its reports should be comprehensive as to geographic range and subject matter. The local media should be tasked to have a flow of programs to bring the data to the public.
* Every metropolis, large and small, needs to have an effective nongovernmental bi-partisan watchdog group, run by citizens interested in comprehensive strategic planning for the metropolis. The Regional Plan Association is one example of scores of such agencies; they exist in New York, San Francisco, Boston, and elsewhere, but there is always room for more.

The data-analysis and watchdog functions are closely related, of course, but the danger is that elected officials from the constituent cities and counties in the metropolis will try to dominate the process, will try to avoid incorporating all the separate general governments into the analyses, and will try to avoid sticky issues, such as the concept of fair housing allocations to suburban communities.

And for whatever reason, sometimes racism being a major but well-obscured factor when discussing participation of suburban agencies in housing, transportation, and zoning practices, the life span of comprehensive region-wide planning and analysis agencies is often shorter than the work requires. A similar fate overtook the extraordinarily useful Advisory Committee on Intergovernmental Relations which, for several decades beginning in the 1960s, provided cogent comparative statistics on federal and state/local fiscal and financial flows; I suspect some of the states did not relish a spotlight on their revenue and expenditure records in an era that was seeing scores of federal categorical programs (devoted to a single subject and often bypassing state channels to give money directly to local governments) consolidated into block grants to be distributed by the states.

The economic base of the metropolis is manifestly the main object of concern for any citizens group or official agency involved in comprehensive planning, and the field is full of complications to be evaluated. The economic base of a relatively small metropolitan area is more subject to fluctuations than the economic base of a major urban agglomeration (to adopt the UN's language). In the 1920s and 1930s, the shift of textile plants from New England cities to the rural South left many cities in New England bereft of their economic base. After World War II, a wide variety of cities in the Midwest lost steel and other forms of manufacturing to firms outside the country, creating the so-called Rust Belt. The creation of the Interstate

Highway System and the growth of air travel and the shift of population from East to West created all sorts of negative pressures on the areas being bypassed by these new forms of transportation or simply left behind. By the end of the twentieth century, the shift of manufacturing and some service industries to Third World countries eroded the economic bases of scores of American cities.

It follows that attention to the economic base is a basic and critical function for both public and private interests. The officials and executives promoting investment in the community and attempting to lure new firms are, of course, expected to tout the good schools, good water, and good environment of the area. With luck some of these attributes attracting newcomers are able to be protected or improved by local efforts; some, however, are clearly controlled by national and international forces, trade, and fiscal policies being among the most significant of all. In short, the metropolitan area in question may not be able to return to its former level of economic activity and must consider a new life, perhaps merely smaller, perhaps seeing opportunities to attract a different population such as retirees or young people tired of city living.

So far as I know, no metropolitan area in America has an empowered central authority to manage its area-wide affairs. At best there will be one or more groups, public and private, that have a truly comprehensive view or strategic plan for the future development of the metropolis; often it is the central city's chamber of commerce that stands in for the whole range of interests and activities involved.

I should like to see some drastically different systems for the future of our metropolises, starting with creation of a metropolis-wide legislative assembly with elected representatives from each of the general governments within its boundaries of the metropolis, and I would like to have this new governmental body given the power to plan improvements to the infrastructure of the area and to tax both people, property, and corporations for implementation of the adopted strategic plan.

Improbable though such a legislative assembly might sound, I think something of the sort will be necessary in the future because I think the various programs run by the federal government that can currently be tapped to provide capital funds for local infrastructure will begin to fade away, partly as a result of lower federal revenues as oil prices remain low while automobiles use less gasoline, thus less money for the highway trust fund. Partly because the feeling will grow that each metropolis has enough of a tax base, if all its constituent governments are included, to build whatever roads and mass facilities are required.

The improvements that are required for convenience also appear to be the ones that contribute to our adjustment to climate change. Among them might be an effective public transit system that deals with suburban sprawl, providing very low-cost door-to-door bus and taxi service as well as large-scale parking facilities at rapid transit stops. All this contributes to improving air quality.

Other improvements might include employer-operated transport systems for employees (such as the door-to-door

Wi-Fi-equipped buses operated by Microsoft); emphasis on safety on the roads; zoning for industrial and residential developments that encourage use of public transport; and an end to prejudice against cluster and multifamily housing developments.

There might also be an emphasis on providing clean water and on keeping sewage and run-off from polluting local water resources. Falling water tables and overtapped rivers make water a vital topic of friction in many metropolises, and one must not underestimate the difficulties at reaching accommodation between types of users in the area, recognizing that water levels are rising and taking whatever action is feasible to protect shoreline developments (but also recognizing that, sometimes, nothing can be done to stem the tide, and removal of buildings from the shore is the only reasonable thing to do)

Perhaps the most important and most intractable issue is the deep-seated racism that permeates US society and thus its metropolises. Ferguson, a prime example of truly bad relations between police and Black neighborhoods, is in the St. Louis metropolitan area and is representative of the issue that must be faced before area-wide changes can be made. Thus any and all work that citizens can do to minimize the impact of racism in the schools, the workplaces, and the official agencies of the local government will contribute to the locality's ability to deal with climate change and increased population in the coming decades.

Final thoughts. We in the United States, deeply committed to our system of relatively autonomous elected local governments, are also sure that central national government ministries should not be the main source of decisions and funds concerning local areas, as happens in most other countries. At the same time, we do not yet have a culture that admits that dealing at the metropolis level, rather than at the city or town level, will be increasingly necessary in the future. Each of us is involved and has responsibility for changing our collective civic behavior, whether we live in a large metropolis, a more vulnerable smaller metropolis, or even in what we can pretend is a rural area that is immune to urban trends. I do not know what it will take to get America to make important substantive changes in our civic society so that we think and act in appropriate metropolitan ways. My hope is that this essay may open some minds to new possibilities or, at minimum, gain some understanding of how we arrived at this point in our nation's history.

Appendix: How Other Nations Deal With Their Local Governments

• • •

THE DETAILS OF HOW A given nation deals with its present set of megacities and how it is preparing for more and bigger such agglomerations in the future are beyond the scope of this essay, assuming that such details could be ascertained; most likely even those on the ground are bewildered and frustrated by the realities of urban settlements surrounding the old central cities. And each of the megacities listed in Chapter 1 is unique, not quite like others in the same nation and defying comparisons with the megacities of other nations.

The country-by-country excerpts concerning local government that presented in this Appendix are intended to show how central governments actually do dominate their local sectors. The quoted material is intended to provide significant insights on a sample of sixteen of the world's countries: I selected four in Asia (China, Japan, India, and Indonesia), four in the Middle East (Egypt, Saudi Arabia, Iran, and Turkey), four in the

Hispanic world (Spain, Mexico, Brazil, and El Salvador) and four in the First World (Russia, Israel, France, and England).

The excerpts (with exceptions noted) come from a website that "contains the on-line versions of books previously published in hard copy by the Federal Research Division of the Library of Congress as part of the Country Studies/Area Handbook Series sponsored by the U.S. Department of the Army between 1986 and 1998. Each study offers a comprehensive description and analysis of the country or region's historical setting, geography, society, economy, political system, and foreign policy." Changes in governments have certainly happened in each of these countries in the intervening years, but I assume that the basic relationships between central and local governments tend to remain as before. The website is reached at http://countrystudies.us.

CHINA

China has two entries in the list of the ten largest megacities: Shanghai ranking third and Beijing eighth. It had fifteen others in the list of all urban agglomerations over 5 million. What we want to understand here is how the governance of its urban agglomerations works.

An exceptionally telling example of the way in which a central government operates in a top-down fashion is the "Jing-Jin-Ji" project centered on Beijing, China's capital and the ninth largest megacity in 2014, to combine four or five provinces abutting Beijing into what *New York Times* writer Ian Johnson, in a series of articles in 2015, calls a supercity or a megalopolis. The area covered is as big as Kansas, he says, and the key to success of the project is rebuilding and extension of very high-speed rail systems. The cost is to be justified by an increase in economic development across the supercity, and, he quotes an expert of Beijing's history who said that the project would require a complete overhaul of governmental operations, including giving local governments the right to levy property taxes.

Capital cities are prime candidates for the kind of immigration that creates much larger populations than the city officials desire but, as reported in one country after another, even in totalitarian states such as pre-1989 soviet republics, it has proved to be impossible to limit in-migrations when better living and better jobs beckon.

It is rare these days to find analyses from mountain to the seas of large watersheds that are the subject area of "regional planning" and "regional science," disciplines that are more academic than applied, but offering a considerable literature for scholars. This "Jing-Jin-Ji" project might be the harbinger of a new trend to make a megacity merely part of an operational regional development program like the Appalachian Program in the United States beginning in the 1950s, which covered 253 counties in a dozen states and emphasized economic development in rural areas as well as improved transportation to and from established cities outside program boundaries.

For our purposes, the "Jing-Jin-Ji" project is a good example of top-down decision-making about the framework for development (perhaps to be expected in all megacities with a country's capital at the core) and leaving a good deal of responsibility in the included provinces to implement the grand strategy. Ian Johnson tells of Beijing taking actions, such as moving activities into nearby "municipalities" (actually provinces, in this case) to begin the leveling out process. The Tianjin Municipality contained one of the earliest and best "New Area" economic development organization and is scheduled to play an important role in the supercity project, but a few weeks after the Johnson article appeared, Tianjin's Binhai New Area hit the news as colossal explosions of warehouses occurred, followed by a scurry for resources from Beijing to handle the damage. Presumably, the "Jing-Jin-Ji" project continues, and here we leave a contemporary story and return to older UN and *Wikipedia* sources.

China's "fundamental principle is democratic centralism under State Constitution…In this respect, all local organs are essentially extensions of central government authorities and thus are responsible to the 'unified leadership' of the central organs…The 1979 reform mandated that the party should not interfere with the administrative activities of local government organs and that its function should be confined to 'political leadership' to ensure that the party's line was correctly followed and implemented."

It is not easy to discover what all the changes in recent decades in China mean for the welfare of people currently living in a megacity, but democracy in the form of meaningful participation by local citizens is not to be expected soon.

JAPAN

Japan drew inspiration from China in the Middle Ages, eventually began to challenge it for domination over East Asia and, as of 2014, has the largest megacity of all, Tokyo, and the seventh largest, Kinki Major Metropolitan, which is centered on Osaka. Among the over-5-million group, Japan has Nagoya thirty-fourth and Kitakyushu sixty-third. The Country Study says:

Japan has a unitary rather than a federal system of government, in which local jurisdictions largely depend on national government both administratively and financially...the postwar Ministry of Home Affairs, as well as other national ministries, has the authority to intervene significantly in regional and local government. The result of this power is a high level of organizational and policy standardization among the different local governments. Because local tax revenues are insufficient to support prefectural

*and city governments, these bodies depend on the cen-
tral government for subsidies...*

The Country Study also suggests that Japan's local governments are not entirely passive. People have a strong
sense of local community, are often suspicious of the central government, and wish to preserve the uniqueness of
their prefecture, city, or town.

INDIA

While Japan has the largest megacity, India has the next
largest, Delhi. India also has Mumbai sixth among the
megacities plus seven areas among the over-5-million
set of urban agglomerations: Kolkata (Calcutta) seventh,
Bangalore thirty-first, Chennai (Madras) thirty-second,
Hyderabad thirty-eighth, Ahmedabad forty-sixth, Pune
(Poona) sixty-first, and Surat sixty-sixth.

The Country Study for India does not provide information about governmental structure and finance, but it
does offer social analysis of growth under conditions that
may apply widely in the "developing world." As for growth
in India: slightly more than 26 percent of the country's
population is urban, and in 1991 more than half of urban
dwellers lived in 299 urban agglomerates or cities of more
than 100,000 people.

The growth of India has continued over the ensu-
ing quarter of a century to the present, much of it "the
result of rural-urban migration, as villagers seek better

lives for themselves in the cities." The scene in these cities is familiar:

> *Congestion, noise, traffic jams, air pollution, and major shortages of key necessities characterize urban life. Every major city of India faces the same proliferating problems of grossly inadequate housing, transportation, sewerage, electric power, water supplies, schools, and hospitals. Slums and jumbles of pavement dwellers' lean-tos constantly multiply. An increasing number of trucks, buses, cars, three-wheel autorickshaws, motorcycles, and motorscooters, all spewing uncontrolled fumes, surge in sometimes haphazard patterns over city streets jammed with jaywalking pedestrians, cattle, and goats. Accident rates are high (India's fatality rate from road accidents, the most common cause of accidental death, is said to be twenty times higher than United States rates)...*

Despite the exterior appearance of chaos, slum life is highly structured, with many economic, religious, caste, and political interests expressed in daily activity. Living conditions are extremely difficult.

INDONESIA

Indonesia, with its capital city Jakarta included as twenty-eighth in the list of megacities is here to represent the rest of Asia as we leave the enormous presences of China, Japan, and

India. Where the Country Studies, as noted, are often notably short on material about local government, the situation in Indonesia was rather different, showing in detail the pyramidal nature of its political system; a few of its comments follow:

> *Government administration is processed through descending levels of administrative subunits. Indonesia is made up of twenty-seven provincial-level units. In 1992 there actually were only twenty-four provinces, including Jakarta...*
>
> *Regional and local governments enjoy little autonomy. Their role is largely administrative: implementing policies, rules, and regulations...The political goal is to maintain the command framework of the unitary state, even at the cost of developmental efficiency. Governments below the national level, therefore, serve essentially as subordinate administrative units through which the functional activities of Jakarta-based departments and agencies reach out into the country.*

EGYPT

We shift to the Middle East cultural zone and to Egypt with Al-qahirah (Cairo) as tenth on the list of megacities and none in the over-5-million class.

Egypt is in a state of turmoil as this was written in 2015, but the Country Study provides a cogent look at the way in which local government in a highly structured society may end up as an important cog in a social system full of corruption and struggles for power.

> *Local government traditionally enjoyed limited power in Egypt's highly centralized state...Sadat took several measures to decentralize power to the provinces and towns. Governors acquired more authority under Law Number 43 of 1979, which reduced the administrative and budgetary controls of the central government over the provinces. The elected councils acquired, at least formally, the right to approve or disapprove the local budget. In an effort to reduce local demands on the central treasury, local government was given wider powers to raise local taxes. But local representative councils became vehicles of pressure for government spending, and the soaring deficits of local government bodies had to be covered by the central government. Local government was encouraged to enter into joint ventures with private investors, and these ventures stimulated an alliance between government officials and the local rich that paralleled the infitah alliance at the national level. Under Mubarak decentralization and local autonomy became more of a reality, and local policies often reflected special local conditions. Thus, officials in Upper Egypt often bowed to the powerful Islamic movement there, while those in the port cities struck alliances with importers.*

SAUDI ARABIA

Saudi Arabia, in turn, provides a look at local government in a Sunni Islamic context, possibly to be compared to its rival Iran. Saudi Arabia has one urban agglomeration with more than 5 million population: Riyadh, number fifty-two. As for the rest:

> *Saudi Arabia consisted of fourteen provinces, or amirates, each governed by an amir (governor) appointed by the king...The governors also served as commanders of the local police and Saudi Arabian National Guard units and supervised the recruitment of local men for these security forces.*
>
> *The mayors of each city, town, and village within an amirate were formally responsible to the Ministry of Municipal and Rural Affairs, although in practice they also were subordinate to the governor.*

I was teaching a graduate course in the law of urban planning in the United States. Two Saudi Arabian students found themselves in the class and considered all of its US content irrelevant to their careers. They went to the dean to demand a course with content on planning in their country rather than in the United States. The resolution was permission to have them do some research about what city planning involved in countries such as theirs; their reports, very briefly, concluded that the only consideration on whether any building project, public or private, could proceed was whether the local imam approved.

IRAN

Tehran, number forty, is Iran's only urban agglomeration over-5-million population. As of 1987, Iran was divided into twenty-four provinces (*ostans*). Each province was subdivided into several counties (*shahrestans*).

> *Prior to the Revolution, the governor general was the most powerful person in each province. Since 1979, however, the clerical imam jomehs, or prayer leaders, have exercised effective political power at the provincial level. The imam jomeh is the designated representative of the faqih in each county...*

So Shiite Iran and Sunni Saudi Arabia appear to have similar systems...

TURKEY

Turkey has Istanbul, number fifty-two, as its major urban agglomeration.

> *Each province is administered by a governor (vagi) appointed by the Council of Ministers with the approval of the president. The governors function as the principal agents of the central government and report to the Ministry of Interior...The constitution also stipulates that the central administration oversee elected local councils in order to ensure the effective provision of local services and to safeguard the public interest.*

...Each provincial capital, each district seat, and each town of more than 2,000 people is organized as a municipality headed by an elected mayor. Government at the provincial level is responsible for implementing national programs for health and social assistance, public works, culture and education, agriculture and animal husbandry, and economic and commercial matters.

SPAIN

On to the Hispanic world and its reliance on the Napoleonic Code for the administration of local affairs. Spain has two entries in the list of seventy-one agglomerations over 5 million: Madrid, number fifty-four, and Barcelona, number sixty-nine.

Institutions of local government have undergone marked transformations since the Franco era, when they functioned primarily as instruments of the central government...

Because of the degree of authority that has been devolved to the autonomous communities from the central government, local institutions are politically dependent on these communities; however, they remain to a large extent financially dependent on Madrid...

Government at the municipal level is administered by a Municipal Council, the members of which are directly elected by universal suffrage and according to proportional representation...The Constitution defines the provinces as territorial divisions "designed to carry out the activities of the central government." The civil governor, who is the highest executive of the state administration at the provincial level, is appointed by the prime minister on the recommendation of the minister of interior.

MEXICO

Mexico, has Ciudad de Mexico (Mexico City) as fourth on the megacity list.

The presidency is the paramount institution, not only of the Mexican state, but of the entire Mexican political system...Much of the aura of presidential power derives from the president's direct and unchallenged control over both the state apparatus and the ruling political party, the PR...

The basic unit of Mexican government is the municipality (municipio), more than 2,000 of which were legally in existence in 1996...

Although they are authorized to collect property taxes and user fees, municipalities have historically lacked the means to do so, relying mainly on transfers from higher levels of government for approximately 80 percent of their revenues.

BRAZIL

Brazil has three members of the over-5-million group: Sao Paulo, fifth; Rio de Janeiro, seventeenth; and Belo Horizonde, fifty-ninth.

The municipalities of Brazil...are administrative divisions of the Brazilian states. At present date, Brazil has 5,570 municipalities, making the average municipality population 34,361. The average state in Brazil has 214 municipalities...

Each municipality has an autonomous local government, comprising a mayor (Prefeito) and a legislative body (Câmara Municipal). Both the local government and the legislative body are directly elected by the population every four years...Each municipality has the constitutional power to approve its own laws and collects taxes and also receives funds from the state and federal governments. However, municipal governments have no judicial power, and courts are only organised at the state or federal level.

El Salvador

There are no areas with a population of more than 5 million.

El Salvador is divided into fourteen administrative divisions called departments, the equivalent of states in the United States. Each department is administered by a governor appointed by the president...

Below the departmental level, El Salvador is divided into 261 municipalities (or municipios, the equivalent of counties in the United States)...

The powers of local government are circumscribed by those of the central government. Because department governors are appointed by the president, their independence is questionable. Despite their status as elected representatives, the powers of municipal officeholders are also limited in certain key areas. The most glaring example is taxation.

ISRAEL

Another nation with no areas with more than 5 million population.

As of late 1988, there were two levels of local government: the central government operated the upper or district level; citizens elected the lower and relatively autonomous municipal level officials. The system of district administration and local government was for the most part based on statutes first promulgated during the Ottoman era and perpetuated under the British Mandate for Palestine and under Yishuv policies. Since independence it has been modified to deal with changing needs and to foster local self-rule. As of late 1988, local government institutions had limited powers, experienced financial difficulties, and depended to a great extent on national ministries; they were, nevertheless, important in the political framework.

Russian Federation

The capital city, Moscow, is twenty-first in the megacity category.

> *The Russian Federation has made few changes in the Soviet pattern of regional jurisdictions. The 1993 constitution establishes a federal government and enumerates eighty-nine subnational jurisdictions, including twenty-one ethnic enclaves with the status of republics. There are ten autonomous regions, or okruga (sing., okrug), and the Jewish Autonomous Oblast (Yevreyskaya avtonomnaya oblast', also known as Birobidzhan). Besides the ethnically identified jurisdictions, there are six territories (kraya; sing., kray) and forty-nine oblasts (provinces). The cities of Moscow and St. Petersburg are independent of surrounding jurisdictions; termed "cities of federal significance," they have the same status as the oblasts. The ten autonomous regions and Birobidzhan are part of larger jurisdictions, either an oblast or a territory .... As the power and influence of the central government have become diluted, governors and mayors have become the only relevant government authorities in many jurisdictions.*

Germany

Another nation with no areas with a population of more than 5 million.

Because Germany has a federal system, state (Land; pl., Länder) and local governments also have important functions. This reflects the German tradition, which before Hitler combined a mix of national, Land, and local structures with carefully defined and deliberately circumscribed powers. Land and even local authorities are involved in many economic functions, such as social services, development and energy policy, education (including vocational training), public housing, environmental protection, and industrial policy. They also share certain tax revenues that are centrally collected but distributed among the central, Land, and local authorities in accordance with carefully negotiated ratios that were changed after unification slightly to the advantage of the new eastern Länder.

FRANCE

The capital city, Paris, is twenty-fifth in the megacity category.

Historically, government authority in France has been highly centralized...For centuries the French monarchy sought to centralize economic and military power to control rebellious members of the nobility in the provinces. The French Revolution of 1789 dismantled the monarchy but retained a highly centralized national administration, centered in Paris. Today this system remains largely in place. Reforms introduced in recent decades have transferred some powers to local authorities, but many of France's major policy decisions are still made in the nation's capital.

ENGLAND

The capital city, London, is twenty-seventh in the set of twenty-nine over-10-million megacities.

Local government in the United Kingdom has origins that predate the United Kingdom itself, as each of the four countries (England, Scotland, Northern Ireland, and Wales) of the United Kingdom has its own separate system.

England gets short shrift in this essay, partly because in 2015 it too had a hierarchal system of planning and revenue generation and more importantly because so much of the US system took shape when the thirteen colonies were becoming somewhat independent of the mother country and thus somewhat unleashed from English common law.

In other words, the colonies and then the states under the Constitution diverged from their roots in England, providing us with a rather different system than anyplace in the world (assuming the world is fairly represented by the sixteen countries we peeked at).

And so at last we arrive at the United States of America and the metropolises it has spawned. A few parting thoughts as we leave the rest of the world to its own devices and return our attention to the United States.

Even for the countries with power over local governments centralized in national ministries, dealing with megacities and their smaller siblings is not easy. As one example, the chief architect in Prague in 1968 told me (just before the Russians took over) that people streamed into the city even though strict controls over its growth had been ordained by the municipal authorities. This is not unlike the process of urbanization elsewhere in the world.

The case of London is also instructive; again and again there have been large-scale reorganizations and reallocations of municipal functions to deal with the region's metropolitan growth, and as an example of how it is often wise to break up large problems (such as transportation within metropolitan boundaries) into smaller chunks, motor-vehicle traffic into central London is strictly controlled. Sooner or later, all the other interrelated aspects of London life will receive comparable degrees of attention, and perhaps the same will be true for the metropolises in the United States.

• • •

About the Author

. . .

Among Alan Rabinowitz's published books are: *Middle Way: Freedom and Progressive Change Since World War II* (Seattle: Quansoo Press, 2012); *Urban Economics and Land Use in America: The Transformation of Cities in the Twentieth Century* (Armonk, NY: M. E. Sharpe, 2004); *Social Change Philanthropy in America* (NY&Westport CT: Quorum/Greenwood Press, 1990); *Land Investment and the Predevelopment Process* (NY&Westport CT: Quorum/Greenwood Press, 1988); *The Real Estate Gamble: Lessons from 50 Years of Boom and Bust* (NY: AMACOM/ American Management Assoc., 1980); *Non-Planning and Redevelopment in Boston: An Analytic Study of the Planning Process* (No. 9, Urban Planning/Development Series, Dept. of Urban Planning, University of Washington, Seattle, 1972); *Municipal Bond Finance and Administration* (NY: Wiley-Interscience, John Wiley & Sons, 1969).

Rabinowitz has worked for governments, large-scale real-estate investment companies, Wall Street bond firms, and a variety of civic and nonprofit organizations and foundations. He served as an officer in the US Navy during the Korean war. Rabinowitz was formerly a professor at the University of Washington in Seattle, teaching state-local finance, housing finance, economic development, and urban planning. He holds an AB from Yale (government), an MBA from Harvard (finance), and a PhD from MIT (city and regional planning). He and his wife, both born in Manhattan, spent their first four decades on the East Coast and moved to Seattle in 1971 with their four teenage children.